INSPIRING STORIES FOR AMAZING GIRLS

*Empowering Tales of Courage,
Confidence, and Kindness*

Katie Wensley

Contents

Introduction

Do you ever feel like life is a tornado that sweeps you off your feet, leaving you unsure how to find solid ground again? At times, it's amazing! Sometimes, it's disappointing. And every so often, it's scary. You're not alone in this world, and there are so many other girls like you who are feeling exactly the way you are right now.

Join me in a world where dreams take flight, friendships blossom in the most unexpected places, and young girls like you discover the power that lies within. Each story in this book is a reminder that no matter where you come from or what you face, you have the strength, creativity, and determination to shape your own future.

You'll meet girls who overcame their fears, stood up for what they believed in, learned the value of kindness, discovered new talents, made lasting friendships, and came to cherish the qualities that make them unique. These aren't just stories of triumph; they are tales of growth, bravery, and the magic that unfolds when you believe in yourself.

As you turn the pages, you may see a bit of yourself in each of these characters, and that's a wonderful thing. I hope you find the inspiration to chase your dreams with passion, face obstacles with courage, and always, always believe in the power of being yourself.

Beyond the Comfort Zone

The sun rose over the quiet suburban neighborhood where Aaliyah Dembay lived. Aaliyah, a 10-year-old girl with wide brown eyes and curly dark brown hair—she got her hair from her father—that framed her light brown face, lay in bed, staring at the ceiling.

Aaliyah loved being outdoors, but today she was feeling off. For years, she'd been swimming and hiking with her family and playing baseball with her friends, yet her heart felt restless.

As Aaliyah dressed in her favorite yellow sundress, she thought about the things she loved—like reading books where the good guys always won, doing jigsaw puzzles with her mom, and watching movies with happy endings. She was always drawn to simple and pure stories in which kindness and goodness triumphed. Lately, even those things didn't seem to fill the space inside her that longed for something new.

The smell of pancakes filled the air, so she bounded downstairs. Aaliyah's mother Krista flipped the golden-brown treats onto a plate. Her father, Tyrese, poured orange juice, and her older brother Josiah, who was 12, was already seated at the table eating.

"Morning, sweet pea," Krista said. She smiled as Aaliyah entered the kitchen.

"Morning, Mom," Aaliyah replied, sliding into her seat across from Josiah. She loved her mom's golden hair, light green eyes, and, most of all, her cheerful nature.

"What's wrong, Aaliyah? You've been quiet lately," Tyrese observed as he sat beside her.

Aaliyah shrugged, poking at her pancake. "I don't know, Dad. I guess I'm just bored."

Josiah snickered. "Bored? How can you be bored when there's baseball to play?"

Aaliyah sighed. "I like swimming and baseball, but it feels like I've been doing the same things forever. I want to try something different."

"Like what?" Krista asked.

Aaliyah hesitated. "Martial arts."

Josiah burst out laughing, nearly choking on his juice. "Martial arts? That's for boys, Aaliyah! You'd get crushed! You're just copying me because I take martial arts!"

"No, I'm not!" Aaliyah replied. She was telling the truth. This had nothing to do with her brother.

Aaliyah's cheeks flushed with embarrassment. She wasn't strong like Josiah, and the idea of stepping into a martial arts class with many boys scared her. But there was also something exciting about it.

"Josiah, that's enough," Tyrese said firmly, giving his son a stern look. "Martial arts isn't just for boys."

"But Dad, I don't want her taking Martial arts with me—" Josiah began, but Krista cut him off.

Josiah didn't argue any further. Aaliyah looked at her parents, feeling hopeful, but the knot of anxiety in her stomach remained. What if Josiah was right? What if she wasn't any good at it?

"Josiah, your sister can try whatever she wants." Krista smiled warmly, brushing a stray curl from Aaliyah's forehead. "You can do anything you set your mind to, sweetie. If you want to learn martial arts, then we'll support you all the way. Just remember, it's not about being the best right away- it's about trying, learning, and growing."

Aaliyah glared at her brother and said, "What if Josiah's right?"

Tyrese reached across the table and took her hand in his. "The only way to find out is to try. No matter what happens, we're proud of you for having the courage to try something new."

Later that day, Aaliyah met up with her best friend Zara at the park. Zara had long, dark hair and an adventurous spirit that always inspired Aaliyah. They found a quiet spot under a tree, where they often sat to talk about everything.

"What's wrong, Aaliyah?" Zara asked, leaning against a tree.

Aaliyah bit her lip, unsure of how to start. But Zara had always been her friend, so she took a deep breath and let the words spill out.

"I've been thinking about trying martial arts," Aaliyah admitted, twisting a strand of her hair nervously. "But I'm scared I won't be any good at it. And Josiah says it's only for boys."

Zara's eyes lit with excitement. "You'd be great at martial arts! Don't listen to Josiah—he's just trying to mess with you."

Aaliyah smiled weakly. "Maybe, but I'm not strong or coordinated. What if they laugh at me?"

Zara shook her head. "Aaliyah, you've always been good at everything you try. You're smart, you're quick, and you've got a big heart. Those are the things that matter. Besides, everyone starts somewhere, right? You don't have to be perfect from the start."

Aaliyah looked down, still uncertain. "I don't know, Zara. I just wish I could be sure that I'd be good at it before I even start."

Zara squeezed Aaliyah's hand. "The only way to find out is to try. And I'll be there to cheer you on."

Aaliyah felt a spark of courage flicker inside. Zara was right. She couldn't let fear hold her back from trying something new. But the thought of *actually* walking into a martial arts studio still made her heart race with anxiety.

That evening, as Aaliyah closed her eyes, she imagined herself as a martial artist, moving with confidence and skill, just like the people she'd seen on TV.

The next day, while Aaliyah walked home after school, her thoughts swirled with everything her parents said the morning before. As she approached the martial arts studio, her steps slowed, and she found herself peering through the large glass windows with curiosity and fear.

Inside, she saw a group of boys her age practicing their moves with serious expressions. They moved with precision, their kicks and punches sharp and controlled. Aaliyah's heart sank; they all seemed so sure of themselves, so strong.

But then, out of the corner of her eye, she spotted someone different. It was a girl about the same age as Aaliyah, with a confident stance and a determined look in her eyes. She was moving just as skillfully as the boys, her movements fluid and precise.

"Wow," she murmured to herself, feeling admiration and anxiety. *Maybe she was just born talented*, Aaliyah suddenly thought, the flicker of hope starting to dim. She sighed and continued her walk home, the image of the confident girl both inspiring and intimidating her.

The next afternoon, as Aaliyah walked past the martial arts studio again, she noticed the same girl—she recognized her from school and thought her name was Emma—practicing inside. This time, Emma caught Aaliyah's gaze, smiled, and waved her over. Aaliyah hesitated. Her heart raced, but something about Emma's friendly smile made her take a step closer.

"Hi, I'm Emma," the girl said as she stepped outside. "I've seen you at school! Are you thinking about joining?"

Aaliyah shifted on her feet, feeling nervous under Emma's kind but curious gaze. "I want to, but my brother says martial arts is only for boys, and I'm not sure if I'll be any good."

Emma's smile widened. "That's nonsense! Martial arts is for everyone. I was terrified the first time I came here, but once I gave it a try, I realized how much I loved it."

Josiah saw Aaliyah on the way to his martial arts lesson. He approached her and frowned when he saw Aaliyah talking to Emma. "Aaliyah, are you really thinking about this? It'll be too hard. I don't think it's your thing."

Emma crossed her arms and gave Josiah a determined look. "And why not? Aaliyah can do anything she puts her mind to, just like anyone else. In fact, I bet she'd be amazing at martial arts."

Josiah looked between the two girls and sighed. "Fine. But don't say I didn't warn you." He walked away snickering.

Emma turned back to Aaliyah, and her bright blue eyes lit with encouragement. "You'll be great, Aaliyah. Don't let anyone tell you otherwise. I'll be there with you, okay?"

Aaliyah smiled. "Okay. I'll give it a try."

The next day after school, Aaliyah stood in front of the martial arts studio with her heart pounding in her chest. She could hear the muffled sounds of practice inside—shouts, thuds, and the rhythmic stomp of feet on the mat. Taking a deep breath, she pushed the door open and stepped inside.

Emma greeted her with a wide grin. "You made it!"

Aaliyah nodded, her stomach doing flip-flops. "I'm ready."

"I'm Mr. Zhiyu Chien, your sensei. I'm glad you're here. Don't be nervous; just do your best," the instructor said as he greeted her.

Aaliyah took her place on the mat, trying to mirror the stances of the other students. As the class began, she felt the initial awkwardness of her movements, but with each passing minute, she grew more focused and tried to follow Mr. Chien's instructions as closely as possible.

As the class progressed, Aaliyah caught on quicker than expected. Her punches grew more precise, her kicks stronger, and a rhythm developed in her movements. To her surprise it felt natural, almost like she'd been doing it for years.

Mr. Chien gave her an encouraging nod. "Very good, Aaliyah. You're picking this up quickly. Keep it up!"

Emma flashed her a thumbs-up from across the room, and Aaliyah couldn't help but smile. The nervousness that had been sitting in her stomach all day slowly melted away, replaced by a growing sense of confidence. She was doing it—she was actually *doing* it. She couldn't wait to tell her parents!

Over the next few weeks, Aaliyah continued to attend her martial arts classes. She no longer felt out of place among the other students; instead, she felt like she belonged. The moves that once seemed difficult were becoming second nature, and she found herself looking forward to each class more and more. Aaliyah felt a familiar buzz of excitement every time she stepped onto the mat in the martial arts dojo.

One day, as Aaliyah progressed through her martial arts routine, she noticed her form was sharper and more precise. She was no longer hesitant or second-guessing herself. Aaliyah realized that she was getting better. It wasn't just about the kicks and punches; it was the confidence growing inside her.

At the end of their lessons, all the students from each class sat on the mat to listen to Mr. Chien's feedback. Aaliyah couldn't help but feel proud when he called her out.

"Aaliyah," Mr. Chien began, "Your progress is remarkable. You've shown great discipline and focus. Keep up the good work."

Aaliyah's heart swelled with pride. She glanced over at Josiah, who was seated at the far edge of the mat. For a moment, their eyes met, and she saw something in his expression that surprised her—pride. But there was also something else that looked a lot like guilt.

After class Aaliyah and Josiah walked home together. Josiah was unusually quiet. Aaliyah couldn't help but wonder what was going on in his mind. Finally, as they reached the park near their house, Josiah stopped and turned to face her.

"Aaliyah," he started, his voice hesitant. "I want to say I'm sorry."

Aaliyah blinked in surprise. "Sorry? For what?"

Josiah looked down, kicking a pebble on the ground. "For what I said before. About martial arts being just for boys. I was wrong."

Aaliyah stared at him, shocked.

"I heard Mr. Chien praising you today," Josiah admitted. "You're really good—way better than I thought you'd be. I just didn't want to admit that my little sister could be better than me."

Aaliyah felt a lump in her throat. "Josiah, it's okay."

"It's not okay," Josiah insisted. "You're amazing at this. I should have supported you from the start. I'm proud of you and want you to keep going, no matter what."

Aaliyah smiled, her heart feeling happy. "Thanks, Josiah. That means a lot."

He grinned at her. "So are you gonna show me how to do some of those moves?"

Aaliyah laughed. "If you can keep up!"

They raced each other home.

That night, as Aaliyah lay in bed, she thought about everything that had happened. She had started martial arts on a whim, not really knowing what to expect. She had been nervous and unsure if she would even like it, let alone be any good at it. But now, she couldn't imagine her life without it. The thrill of learning something new, the satisfaction of getting better, and the pride she felt in herself were all more than she had ever expected.

Aaliyah realized that stepping out of her comfort zone had led her to discover something wonderful—not just a new skill but a new passion. And she now had a new friend in Emma, one of the popular girls at her school.

Aaliyah was no longer the shy girl who doubted herself at every turn. She had learned that she could be strong, that she could excel at something if she put her mind to it, and, more importantly, that gender didn't determine what she could achieve.

> *Aaliyah's story shows the power of stepping out of your comfort zone. She overcame her doubts and fears and discovered a new passion for martial arts. Aaliyah learned that trying something new can lead to unexpected joy and self-confidence. This teaches us that we can achieve anything if we're willing to take a chance, regardless of others' opinions.*

The Paws of Kindness

S hellene Moffatt stared out the window of her room, watching the rain fall. She sighed, feeling the familiar pang of loneliness, and played with a strand of her short, naturally blond hair. At nine years old, Shellene often felt like a misfit. Adopted and an only child, she struggled to connect with others her age. Her parents, loving and supportive as they were, couldn't quite fill the void she felt inside.

Shellene spotted a tiny, shivering kitten huddled under a bush in their front yard as she looked out the window. Her heart went out to the little creature.

She dashed outside with an umbrella, scooped up the kitten, and rushed back into the house. The kitten was soaking wet, its fur matted and dirty, but it was the most beautiful thing Shellene had ever seen.

"Mom! Dad! Look what I found!" Shellene called out, cradling the kitten in her arms.

Her parents, Donna and Greg, hurried into the living room. Donna's eyes widened at the sight of the disheveled kitten. "Oh, Shellene, you found a stray!"

"We need to take care of it," Shellene insisted, her bright blue eyes pleading.

Greg smiled gently. "All right, let's get it cleaned up first."

Together, they bathed the kitten, who turned out to be a delicate Siamese with striking blue eyes. Shellene named it Smudge and immediately felt a connection she'd never experienced before. Smudge seemed to sense her need for companionship, curling up on her lap and purring contentedly.

The next few days were some of the happiest Shellene had ever known. Smudge became her constant companion, sleeping beside her at night and following her around during the day. She no longer felt so alone. But as much as she loved Smudge, she knew deep down that the kitten might belong to someone else.

One evening, as they sat around the dinner table, Donna brought up the subject that Shellene had been dreading. "Sweetheart, we need to find out if Smudge belongs to someone. It's the right thing to do."

Shellene's heart sank. "But what if no one claims her?"

"Then we can keep her," Greg reassured her. "But we have to try."

Reluctantly, Shellene agreed. The next day, Donna helped her make signs. They printed pictures of Smudge and wrote, "Found Kitten: Siamese, very friendly. Please call if she belongs to you." Together, they put up the signs around the neighborhood. Shellene secretly hoped no one would call.

Shellene's heart would race each time the phone rang, as she feared the call was someone claiming Smudge. But the days went by and no one called about the cat. Shellene started to feel a glimmer of hope that maybe Smudge would stay with her forever.

Time passed, and Smudge became a part of the family. Shellene's parents even bought a small leash, and Shellene started taking Smudge out for little walks up and down the street. On one of these walks, she ran into their elderly neighbor, Elva Novak.

Elva, a kind woman with silver hair and warm eyes, smiled as she saw Shellene and the kitten. "What a beautiful kitten you have there, Shellene."

"Thank you, Mrs. Novak," Shellene replied, beaming. "Her name is Smudge."

Elva's smile faltered slightly. "She looks just like my kitten. I lost her a few weeks ago."

Shellene's heart sank. "Is she a Siamese?"

Elva nodded. "Yes, she is. Her name is Misty. I got her to keep me company after my husband passed away six months ago."

Tears welled up in Shellene's eyes as she realized what she had to do. "I think Smudge might be Misty. I found her a few weeks ago in my yard."

Elva looked at Shellene with a mixture of sadness and gratitude. "Oh, Shellene, thank you for taking such good care of her."

Reluctantly, Shellene handed the leash to Elva. "Here, Mrs. Novak. You should have her back."

Elva took the leash, her eyes misting over. "Oh my goodness, you are such a kind girl, Shellene. I really appreciate you finding my kitten and keeping her safe. You can come visit Misty anytime you want."

Shellene nodded, feeling a lump in her throat. She watched as Elva walked away with the kitten, feeling an ache in her heart. But she knew she had done the right thing.

The next day, Shellene knocked on Elva's door. The older woman answered with a warm smile. "Hello, Shellene. Come in."

Shellene followed Elva into the house, where Misty—formerly Smudge— was lounging comfortably on the couch. The kitten looked up and purred at the sight of Shellene. After petting Misty for awhile, Shellene looked up happily at Elva. Elva noticed the joy in Shellene's eyes and said, "Would you like to help me in the garden?"

Shellene nodded eagerly. She followed Elva outside, and they spent the afternoon tending to the flowers and vegetables. Shellene found that she loved gardening, and even more, she enjoyed spending time with Elva. They talked about everything—from Elva's late husband to Shellene's school life. For the first time in a long while, Shellene felt a sense of belonging.

Days turned into weeks, and Shellene's visits to Elva became a regular occurrence. She helped with the gardening, played with Misty, and listened to Elva's stories. In return, Elva taught her about plants and flowers, sharing her wisdom and experience. Shellene realized that not only did she gain a new friend in Elva, but she also found a passion for gardening.

One sunny afternoon, as they were planting marigolds, Elva looked at Shellene and said, "You know, dear, kindness can change the world."

Shellene paused, thinking about Elva's words. "What do you mean?"

Elva smiled. "If you hadn't been kind enough to give Misty back, we wouldn't have become friends. You've brought so much joy into my life, Shellene. Sometimes, small acts of kindness can make a big difference."

Shellene smiled, feeling a warmth in her heart. She realized that even though she didn't have her own kitten anymore, she had gained something even more precious—a friend and a sense of purpose. She no longer felt like a misfit. She had found her place in the world, and it was filled with kindness and love.

From that day on, Shellene made it her mission to spread kindness wherever she went. She volunteered at the local animal shelter, helped her neighbors with their gardens, and always looked out for those who needed a friend. Through it all, she remembered Elva's words, knowing that her small acts of kindness could indeed change the world.

Shellene's parents watched with pride as their daughter blossomed. Donna often joined Shellene on her visits to Elva's, and they would all share tea and stories together. Greg would sometimes come along too, bringing homemade cookies or lending a hand with heavier gardening tasks. The bond between the Moffatts and Elva grew strong, creating a little close-knit community that supported one another.

One particularly memorable day, Shellene and Elva decided to organize a neighborhood garden party. They had spent weeks preparing, inviting neighbors and friends and decorating Elva's garden with colorful flowers and fairy lights. On the day of the party, the garden was a magical sight, with vibrant blooms and the scent of fresh flowers filling the air.

Neighbors arrived with dishes to share, and the garden buzzed with laughter and conversation. Shellene moved through the crowd, greeting everyone with a smile and feeling a sense of accomplishment and happiness she had never known before. Misty, who wore a little flower crown Shellene had made, pranced around, charming all the guests.

As the sun began to set, Shellene found herself sitting with Elva on a cozy bench in the garden, watching the fairy lights twinkle. Elva patted Shellene's hand and said, "You've brought so much light into this garden and into my life, Shellene. I'm so grateful for you."

Tears of joy filled Shellene's eyes. "I'm grateful for you too, Mrs. Novak. You've taught me so much and made me feel like I belong."

Elva hugged Shellene tightly. "You do belong, my dear. You belong right here where kindness grows."

In the months and years that followed, Shellene continued to nurture her love for gardening and her commitment to kindness. She grew into a compassionate young woman, always ready to lend a helping hand and spread joy wherever she went. And every time she visited Elva, they would sit together in the garden, surrounded by the beauty they had created together, knowing that their friendship was a testament to the power of kindness.

> *Shellene's story shows that small acts of kindness can create powerful connections. By returning the lost kitten, Shellene found a lifelong friend in her elderly neighbor, Elva. Through this bond, she discovered a sense of belonging and purpose. This teaches us that kindness not only helps others but also brings unexpected joy and fulfillment into our own lives.*

United We Rise

K iana Nakamura loved the way the volleyball felt as it hit her hands, and
the satisfying smack that echoed across the gym. Volleyball was more
than just a sport to her- it was where she felt strong, confident, and connected
to her friends. Since moving to Burlington, Vermont, six years ago from
Hawaii, volleyball had become her anchor. It was a place where she could
truly be herself.

Lately, Kiana's team had been struggling. After a series of tough matches,
their spirits were at an all-time low. Kiana's best friend, Tamara, usually the

vibrant spark of the group, had begun to lose some of her shine. Cora, the tallest girl on the team with her long blond hair and gray eyes, was the biggest worrier of them all. If there was something to be anxious about, Cora found it.

One evening after practice, Kiana flopped onto the couch at home, pulling her long black hair out of its usual ponytail and feeling the weight of her team's frustration. Her mom, Mikala, noticed immediately.

"What's wrong, sweetheart?" Mikala asked, sitting down beside her daughter.

Kiana sighed and hugged a throw pillow. "The team's not doing so well, Mom. We're losing matches, and everyone's starting to give up. Even Tamara is losing her confidence, and Cora, well, she's Cora. She's always worrying about everything."

Mikala gently squeezed Kiana's shoulder. "That sounds tough. But I know you, Kiana. You're a natural leader. What do you think needs to change?"

Kiana thought for a moment, chewing on her bottom lip. "I think we need to boost our morale, but I don't know how. I don't know where to start."

Just then, Kiana's dad, Hale, walked into the room. He had overheard the conversation and joined them, sitting on the edge of the coffee table across from Kiana.

"I used to play many sports when I was your age," Hale began, a smile playing at the corners of his mouth. "When my team was in a slump, we didn't give up. We found ways to lift each other up and work through it together."

Kiana perked up, listening intently. "What did you do, Dad?"

Hale leaned in and shared his wisdom. "First, we celebrated small wins. Even if it was just one good play in a match, we'd make a big deal out of it. We also did team bonding activities that didn't involve the sport we were playing— just to build trust and get to know each other better."

Kiana nodded, absorbing every word. "What else?"

"We gave each other constructive feedback. It's important to be honest but also kind. We set clear goals, both as individuals and as a team. We made sure everyone knew their strengths and how they could contribute."

Mikala chimed in, "And remember, recognizing effort is just as important as results. Celebrate how hard everyone is working, not just the wins."

Hale added, "Encourage communication. Make sure everyone feels heard. Sometimes, a pep talk or a good cheer can go a long way. But most importantly, foster a culture of respect and trust. You can't win if you don't trust your teammates."

Kiana's mind was racing with ideas. "That's it! I know what I need to do. Thanks, Mom and Dad!"

The next day at practice, Kiana gathered the team together before they hit the court.

"Hey, everyone," Kiana started, her voice strong and confident. "I know things have been tough lately, but I believe in us. We're a great team, and I think we just need a little boost to get back on track."

Tamara, who was usually brimming with energy, looked up, curious. "What do you have in mind, Kiana?"

Kiana smiled. "I talked to my dad, and he gave me some ideas. What if we start by celebrating our small wins? Like, every time we make a good play, we hype it up. And I think we should do some team bonding activities— something that will help us trust each other—trust falls or other fun exercises that aren't about volleyball."

Cora, who had been quietly listening, frowned slightly. "But what if we mess up? What if it doesn't work?"

Kiana walked over to Cora and placed a reassuring hand on her shoulder. "That's exactly why we need to do this. We have to focus on what we're doing right, not what could go wrong. We're in this together."

Tamara nodded enthusiastically, her energy slowly returning. "I'm in. Let's do this!"

The team agreed, and Kiana suggested they add another weekly practice dedicated solely to teamwork and trust-building. It wasn't just about volleyball anymore; it was about rebuilding their bond as a team.

During their first teamwork practice, Kiana explained one of the exercises: "Okay, for this one, we're going to do trust falls. You stand in front of someone, back-to-front, and then the person in the front falls backward, trusting that your partner will catch you. It's all about trust."

Cora's eyes widened. "What if they don't catch me?"

Tamara, standing next to Cora, grinned. "That's the point. We have to trust each other."

Despite Cora's initial hesitation, she eventually paired up with Tamara, who was quick to offer her infectious smile.

"You got this, Cora. I won't let you fall," Tamara reassured her.

Slowly, Cora leaned back, body stiff with fear, and then she let herself fall. Just as she was about to panic, Tamara caught her, steady and strong. Cora let out a breath she didn't realize she was holding and smiled.

"See? We're in this together," Tamara said, her voice warm.

As the weeks passed, the team continued their special practices, focusing on stamina, agility, and their bond. They ran laps for endurance and did agility drills, box jumps, planks, and lunge twists. Every time someone completed a drill, the others would cheer them on, their voices echoing in the gym, filling it with a new sense of determination.

Kiana could see the difference. Tamara's energy was back and brighter than ever. Cora, while still prone to worry, was starting to smile more as her confidence slowly grew. The entire team felt more connected, more like a family.

Then it happened. The team faced their next match with a new resolve. They communicated better on the court, trusted each other's moves, and celebrated every point, no matter how small. It wasn't just about winning; it was about playing together as one unit.

After a particularly intense rally, Kiana made a perfect set, and Tamara spiked the ball with all her might. The ball hit the ground on the opponent's side, earning Kiana's team the final point in the match.

The gym erupted in cheers. The team hugged each other, laughing and celebrating their hard-fought victory. For the first match in a long time, they felt like a real team again.

That evening, Kiana invited Tamara and Cora over to her house to celebrate. As they walked through the door, Kiana's parents greeted them with warm smiles.

"So, how's the team doing?" Mikala asked, handing them glasses of lemonade.

Kiana beamed, her eyes sparkling with pride. "We won! But it's more than that, Mom. We've been working on our teamwork, just like Dad said. We added an extra weekly practice just to focus on trust and communication. It's really made a difference."

Tamara, her smile as bright as ever, chimed in, "Yeah, we even did trust falls! And Cora, who was super nervous about it at first, totally rocked it!"

Cora blushed, but her smile had a hint of pride. "It was actually kind of fun. And it helped me realize that maybe things won't always go wrong."

Hale, who had been listening quietly, nodded approvingly. "That's great to hear, girls. I'm really proud of you for sticking together and finding a way to lift each other up. That's what being a team is all about."

Mikala added, "And remember, the work doesn't stop here. Keep supporting each other, and you'll continue to grow stronger as a team."

Kiana looked at her parents, her heart swelling with gratitude. "Thanks, Mom. Thanks, Dad. We couldn't have done it without you."

As the season progressed, the team continued to improve. They won match after match, each victory sweeter than the last. They didn't win every game, but when they lost they didn't lose hope. They stuck together as a team. And when they finally made it to the finals of the tournament, they were ecstatic. They had worked hard, not just on their skills, but on their bond as a team.

The day of the finals arrived, and the team huddled together before the match, nerves buzzing with anticipation.

Kiana looked around at her teammates, feeling a surge of pride. "No matter what happens out there today, I'm proud of us. We've come so far, and we've done it together."

Tamara grinned, and her infectious energy lit up the group. "Let's do this, team!"

Cora, her voice steady and confident, added, "Yeah, let's show them what we're made of."

The match was intense, with both teams fighting hard for every point. But Kiana's team was different now. They trusted each other, communicated well, and celebrated every small victory along the way.

When the final whistle blew, they had won. They had achieved the ultimate victory.

A few weeks after their victory, Kiana received an unexpected call from their coach, Mr. Reynolds, who asked to meet her at the gym. When she arrived, he looked more serious than usual.

"Kiana, I've just been informed that our team has been selected to compete in an out-of-state tournament next month," Mr. Reynolds said. "It's a huge opportunity, but there's a catch. We'll be facing some of the best teams in the country, and we're going to need to up our game if we want to stand a chance."

Kiana felt excited and anxious. "Do you think we're ready for this?"

Mr. Reynolds gave her a knowing smile. "I think with the right preparation, you can be. But it's going to require a lot of hard work, and I'm going to need you to help keep the team motivated."

Kiana nodded, determined. "We're up for the challenge, Coach."

One afternoon, Kiana returned home from practice to find her older cousin, Keoni, waiting for her in the living room. Keoni now lived nearby but had been a star volleyball player back in Hawaii, and he was someone Kiana had always looked up to.

"Kiana! Look at you, all grown up and leading your team to victory!" Keoni exclaimed, pulling her into a bear hug.

Kiana laughed, surprised and delighted to see him. "Keoni! What are you doing here?"

Keoni grinned. "I heard about your upcoming tournament, and I thought I'd come by and give you some pointers. I know how much this means to you."

Over the next few days, Keoni helped Kiana and the team refine their skills, sharing tips and techniques that helped him in his own career. His presence gave Kiana a renewed sense of confidence and motivation.

The night before they left for the tournament, Kiana invited the team over to her house for a pre-tournament dinner. Mikala and Hale prepared a feast, and the team sat together, sharing stories and laughing. The nervous energy from earlier in the week melted away.

As they finished dessert, Hale stood up, holding a glass of sparkling cider. "I just want to say how proud I am of all of you. You've worked hard to get here, and no matter what happens tomorrow, you should be proud of yourselves too. Remember, it's not just about winning—it's about playing with heart and supporting each other."

Kiana raised her glass, her voice strong and clear. "To us. To teamwork, to friendship, and to giving it our all tomorrow."

The team clinked their glasses together with their spirits high.

The tournament was tougher than any match they'd faced before. The opposing teams were skilled, and the competition was fierce. Kiana's team struggled in the first game, their nerves getting the better of them.

During a timeout, Kiana gathered them together. "Listen, we didn't come this far to give up now. We know what we're capable of, and we've faced tough challenges before. Let's show them what we're made of!"

The team rallied, and as they stepped back onto the court, their energy shifted. They played with everything they had, trusting each other's abilities and cheering each other on with every point.

Though the final game was close, they ultimately lost by just a few points. But as they gathered together, sweaty and exhausted, Kiana realized that they'd won something much more important—a deeper bond and a sense of pride in how far they'd come.

As they left the court, the team huddled together one last time, their heads held high.

"We may not have won the tournament," Kiana said, "but we've won as a team. And that's something no one can take away from us."

> *Kiana learned that true strength in a team comes from trust, communication, and celebrating small victories. By focusing on building morale and supporting one another, Kiana and her volleyball team rediscovered their confidence and bond, and it led to greater success. This story reminds us that unity and perseverance can overcome challenges and make every effort count, win or lose.*

Courage on Wheels

Sofia Russo's sneakers squeaked against the shiny linoleum floor of the school hallway as she practically skipped toward the cafeteria. Her long chestnut-brown hair bounced behind her in a neat ponytail, and her dark brown eyes sparkled with excitement. Today Mrs. Ransen announced that the sign-up sheet for the school talent show would be posted soon, and Sofia couldn't wait to tell her best friend, Lucy Blackwood.

As Sofia rounded the corner, she spotted Lucy by their usual lunch table. Lucy's blond hair was naturally wavy and sat on her shoulders. Her bright blue eyes, normally filled with mischief, seemed unusually dull. It wasn't like Lucy to look so serious, and Sofia's heart sank as she approached.

"Hey, Luce!" Sofia greeted her cheerfully as she plopped on the bench beside Lucy. "Did you hear? The talent show sign-up sheet is going up soon! Are you going to enter?"

Lucy looked up, a small smile playing on her lips, but it didn't reach her eyes. "I don't know if I'm going to sign up this year, Sof."

Sofia blinked in surprise. "What? But you love performing! Why wouldn't you sign up?"

Lucy shrugged. "Because all anyone will see is this." She gestured to her wheelchair with a resigned sigh. "No one will even pay attention to what I'm doing. They'll just see the girl in the wheelchair and nothing else."

Sofia frowned. "That's not true, Lucy. You're funny, you're smart, and you've got so much talent! You can do anything you want. You did your baton routine last year, didn't you?" She looked at Lucy's wheelchair. "I'm such a bad friend. I got so caught up in the excitement that I forgot that this time last year was before the car accident and you weren't in a wheelchair. I'm so sorry! Maybe you can't do your baton routine, but there's definitely something else you can do instead."

Lucy looked away, her voice barely a whisper. "I want to be a comedian, Sofia. But who's going to take me seriously? They'll just laugh because they think I'm a joke. My legs are paralyzed. I can't even walk around on the stage as I talk."

Sofia reached out and placed a hand on Lucy's. "Lucy, making people laugh is your superpower. You always say how happy it makes you when others are smiling. You have to share that with everyone! You won't know what people will think until you try."

Lucy sighed, still not convinced. "But what if they don't laugh? What if I mess up?"

Sofia grinned, squeezing her hand. "You're the funniest person I know, Lucy. You've got this!"

That evening, Sofia found herself sitting on her bed, her favorite book in hand, but she wasn't turning the pages. Her older sister Nina walked by the room and noticed Sofia's distant staring.

"What's wrong, Sofia? You're usually buried in that book. Something on your mind?"

Sofia looked up, her dark eyes troubled. "It's Lucy. She wants to be in the talent show, but she's scared. She thinks everyone will just see her wheelchair and not her talent. How can I help her?"

Nina sat beside Sofia, wrapping an arm around her shoulders. "You're already helping just by being there for her. But maybe you can give her a little push. Why not go with her to put her name on the sign-up sheet? And maybe offer to be help her with her act, or even offer to be a part of her act, so she won't be alone up there."

Sofia's eyes lit up as she nodded. "That's a great idea, Nina! Thanks!"

The next day, during their lunch break, Sofia and Lucy made their way to the talent show sign-up sheet. Sofia eagerly wrote her name down next to "Gymnastics Dance," and a smile spread across her face as she handed the pen to Lucy.

Lucy hesitated, staring at the pen like it was a venomous snake. "I can't do it, Sofia. I'm too scared."

Sofia turned to her with a determined look. "You have every right to participate, just like everyone else. And I'd love to help you with your act. You can do this. You're great." Lucy hesitated for a long time then suddenly grabbed the pen, reached forward, and wrote her name down on the sheet under "Comedy."

Just then, a group of students approached the sign-up sheet. Jillian, a girl with flowing auburn hair who was known for her love of poetry, wrote her name down for a poem recital. Manny, a tall boy with a confident stride, signed up for basketball dribbling, while Rohan, who always had a trick up his sleeve, listed his act as magic tricks.

As they finished signing up, Jillian turned to Lucy with a smirk. "What's your talent, Lucy? Wheelchair racing?"

Manny and Rohan snickered, and the trio walked away, leaving Lucy deflated. "See?" she whispered to Sofia. "They won't even see what I'm doing. They'll only see the wheelchair."

Sofia clenched her fists, anger bubbling up inside her at the bullies. "Come to my place after school," Sofia said firmly. "We're going to work on your act, and I know you'll blow everyone away."

Lucy reluctantly agreed. That afternoon, they found themselves in Sofia's living room, as Lucy nervously fiddled with her wheelchair's armrest.

"Okay, Luce, hit me with your best jokes," Sofia said, settling down on the floor, her hair fanning out around her.

Lucy hesitated and then began. Her voice was shaky at first but grew stronger as she continued. As Lucy delivered punchline after punchline, Sofia burst into laughter. The sound filled the room and lifted Lucy's spirits.

Nina, who had been listening from the doorway, joined them. "You've got great timing, Lucy. Just remember to make eye contact with your audience and keep them engaged."

The next day, Sofia and Lucy went to the school auditorium to practice. But there was a major problem—there was no ramp for Lucy to get onto the stage.

"This isn't fair," Sofia muttered, her frustration evident as she paced the empty auditorium. "You need to be able to get up there just like everyone else."

Determined, Sofia marched to Mrs. Ransen's classroom after school. "Mrs. Ransen, we need a ramp for the stage in the auditorium. Lucy can't perform if she can't get on the stage."

Mrs. Ransen smiled warmly at Sofia. "Thank you for bringing this to my attention, Sofia. I'll make sure a ramp is installed before the talent show."

True to her word, a few days later, a ramp was added to the stage. Sofia and Lucy tested it out, with Lucy rolling confidently onto the stage and her fears slowly melting away.

Even with the ramp, Lucy was still nervous. "Sofia, I'm not sure I can do this," Lucy admitted one afternoon. "I'm afraid of being up there all by myself."

Sofia put a reassuring hand on Lucy's shoulder. "Then let's make it a team act. If you use props, I'll come onstage with you and hand them to you during your act. That way, you won't be alone."

Lucy's eyes lit up with hope. "You'd do that for me?"

"Absolutely," Sofia replied without hesitation.

With renewed determination, they practiced together every day, fine-tuning Lucy's act. Sofia helped Lucy choose the right props, and by the end of the week, Lucy felt confident and excited for the big day.

Finally, the day of the talent show arrived. The auditorium buzzed with energy as students and teachers filled the seats, eager to see the performances.

Sofia's gymnastic dance for the talent show was an energetic performance that blended dance with powerful gymnastics. It went very well, and the audience seemed to like it. Sofia had been excited to perform her act, but was way more excited to help Lucy.

After her act, Sofia found Lucy backstage. Lucy was a bundle of nerves, her hands trembling as she adjusted her props.

Sofia knelt beside her, her voice gentle but firm. "Lucy, you've got this. Remember, making people laugh is your superpower. Just go out there and show them what you can do. I will be right beside you."

Lucy took a deep breath and nodded. "Okay. Let's do this."

When Lucy's turn came, Sofia rolled Lucy onto the stage, and the bright lights shone down on them. Sofia knew Lucy's heart was pounding in her chest as she faced the audience, but Sofia could tell it was helping that she was on the stage with her friend.

Taking a deep breath, Lucy launched into her act. She started with a joke about school lunches, then moved on to funny observations about their teachers. The audience began to chuckle, and as Lucy continued, their laughter grew louder. Throughout the act, Sofia handed Lucy her props and smiled at her friend encouragingly every chance she got.

The more the audience laughed, the more confident Lucy became. Her jokes flowed effortlessly, and soon the entire auditorium was filled with laughter. Sofia's heart swelled with pride as her best friend shone in the spotlight.

By the time Lucy delivered her final punchline, the audience was roaring with laughter and applause. Lucy beamed, her face glowing with happiness. She had done it—she had conquered her fears and won over the crowd.

After all the performances were finished, the judges announced the winners. Sofia's gymnastics dance took third and Rohan's magic show came in second. Lucy's comedic act took first place! The entire auditorium erupted in applause as Lucy wheeled forward to accept her trophy with a smile brighter than ever.

As students and teachers crowded around to congratulate Lucy, Sofia couldn't help but feel a sense of fulfillment. Jillian, Manny, and Rohan were among the first to approach Lucy. Their earlier teasing was forgotten as they praised her performance.

"You were amazing, Lucy," Jillian said sincerely, her eyes full of admiration. "I've never laughed so hard in my life."

"Yeah, you totally killed it," Rohan said with a grin. "I think we'll see your name in lights one day."

Lucy blushed and replied, "Thank you for your kind words. I was so nervous."

"Don't I know it," Rohan agreed. "I was sick in the boy's room just before I went on. I hope I can eliminate the stage fright if I do some shows in the future."

Lucy turned to Rohan. "Wait! You have stage fright?"

Rohan's eyes lifted. "For sure. It's awful."

"Me too," Jillian said, nodding in agreement. "It's nerve-wracking to be up there all alone. You're so lucky you had Sofia with you. That was super smart."

"It did make it easier," Lucy said.

"See, you're just like everyone else," Sofia reassured Lucy, happy that their classmates were sharing their feelings to make Lucy feel better.

As Sofia watched Lucy interact with Rohan, Jillian, and Manny, she couldn't help but be incredibly happy for her friend. She thought about how everyone deserves a chance to shine. Sofia was glad that Lucy had won first place and thought about how she had helped her win. It made her feel good inside that she could help Lucy realize her dreams, and she was happy that her best friend felt included and important.

"Why don't we celebrate at my house after school?" Sofia suggested. Lucy enthusiastically agreed.

On their way to Sofia's, Lucy said, "Thank you for all of your help, Sofia. I couldn't have done this without you."

"Of course you could have. You're much stronger than you think you are," Sofia encouraged her. "But next year, I'll try harder because I want first place."

"You'll have to beat me first," Lucy said with a grin.

"That sure will be tough, but I'm up for the challenge."

Lucy's smile didn't disappear for the rest of the evening, and neither did Sofia's.

Sofia helped her best friend Lucy overcome her fears and realize her talent for comedy, despite being nervous about performing in a wheelchair. The story shows that true friendship means supporting one another through challenges, and that everyone deserves a chance to shine. By believing in Lucy, Sofia proved that, with encouragement and determination, you can be brave even when you feel afraid.

The Science of Truth

Adaline Chevalier sat at her desk, her fingers nervously tapping on the edge of her notebook and twisting her long light-brown hair. Her gray eyes flickered with frustration. She had just turned 12 and was one of the brightest kids in her class, but when Mrs. Levine, her teacher, announced the upcoming science fair, and the entire class erupted in cheers, Adaline let out a low, frustrated moan.

"The science fair competition will take place in a month," Mrs. Levine continued, her voice full of excitement. "It's time to start thinking about your projects." Adaline slumped in her seat. The science fair was in a month?

Science was one of her favorite subjects, but science projects? They always filled her with dread. No matter how hard she tried, she could never think of a good idea, and, this year, she was determined to win. Last year, her rival, Andrew Roberts, had taken home first place with his elaborate volcano model, and Adaline was determined not to let him win again.

As the school day ended, and the students filed out of the classroom, Adaline's best friend Piper Dixxon caught up with her. Piper, with her wild, curly black hair and rebellious spirit, was the kind of person who never let anything get her down.

"What's up, Addie? You look like you just lost a million dollars," Piper said, her bright green eyes sparkling with curiosity.

Adaline sighed. "It's the science fair. I have no idea what to do. And Andrew—he's so smug about winning last year. I can't let him beat me again!"

Piper frowned. "Ugh, he thinks he's so smart. Whatever you do, don't let him win again. We've got to think of something."

The two girls spent the next few hours brainstorming ideas, but nothing seemed right. Piper suggested a crystal garden, but Adaline shook her head. "Andrew's going to come up with something even better. I need something unique, something that will blow everyone away."

When she arrived home, her mother, Collette, immediately noticed her mood. "What's wrong, my love?" she asked, her voice full of concern.

Adaline sighed and threw herself onto the couch. "It's the science fair, Mom. I can't think of what to do."

Her father, Pierre, who was in the kitchen preparing dinner, overheard the conversation and joined them. "Why not do a project with batteries? Or maybe something with magnets?" he suggested, always eager to help with ideas.

Adaline liked some of his suggestions, but she couldn't decide. "I don't know, Dad. I want to do something different, something amazing."

The next day at school, Piper was waiting for her at their usual spot by the lockers.

"Any luck with the science project?" Piper asked.

Adaline shook her head. "Not yet."

Piper frowned. "Just don't let Andrew win."

As the day dragged on, Adaline couldn't shake the feeling of impending failure. By the end of the day, she was no closer to a solution and was feeling more anxious than ever.

That evening, after a frustrating attempt to come up with a project on her own, Adaline was relieved when her mom knocked on her door.

"I've got an idea," Collette announced, holding up a notebook filled with sketches and notes. "How about a project on the different ways plants respond to light? You could use different colored lights to see how it affects their growth."

Adaline's eyes lit up. "That *does* sounds interesting. Thanks, Mom. Let me think about it for a bit."

Collette smiled, happy to help. "I thought it might help you learn more about something you already love."

Adaline thought about her mom's idea for the rest of the night. It made sense, since she loved plants and gardening so much. And it would help her learn more about her favorite hobby.

Adaline finally decided to go with her mom's idea and was determined to make it work. She spent the next few weeks working on her project in the living room and carefully setting up her experiment. Small pots with seedlings in them were lined up under makeshift light structures—one with a red bulb, another with a blue bulb, and a third with a regular white bulb. She diligently recorded the results as the plants slowly grew and changed. But no matter what she tried, the plants didn't seem to respond the way she had hoped. The leaves remained stubbornly the same, showing no significant difference in growth under the various lights.

"Ugh, this isn't working," she said out loud, frustrated. "They're supposed to show something by now!"

With the science fair deadline looming, panic set in. She fidgeted with her pencil and bit her lip as she looked at her plants, which all seemed to be about the same size. Her mind raced, thinking about her classmates and her teacher and how she desperately wanted to impress everyone with her project.

She stared at the chart, which was currently blank except for the headings "Red Light," "Blue Light," and "White Light." She picked up her pencil and tapped it against the paper as an idea formed in her mind.

"Well, it's just a little tweak. Everyone already knows red light is supposed to make plants grow taller, right?"

Desperate to win and terrified of failing, Adaline made a decision. She concocted fake results and altered her data to make it look as if her experiment had been a success. She scribbled down her "results" for the red light column, writing that those plants grew the strongest. For the blue light, she wrote that the plants grew slower but had thicker stems, and for the white light, she wrote that they grew at a normal pace.

She stepped back, looking at her work, then at the plants. Her heart beat a little faster. "It's just what everyone expects. It's not like they'll notice anyway." She wrote down her fake results on a posterboard and drew fake pictures of the plants. At first, she felt a sense of triumph, but it was quickly overshadowed by a gnawing guilt that she couldn't shake.

The night before the science fair, Adaline lay in bed and stared at the ceiling. The weight of her deception pressed down on her like a heavy blanket, making it impossible to sleep. She tried to convince herself that it didn't matter, that no one would find out, but, deep down, she knew she was lying to herself.

The day of the science fair arrived, and Adaline stood nervously by her project as her classmates and teachers walked around the room, examining the various experiments. Andrew was at the far end of the room, proudly showing off his project on electromagnetism.

When Mrs. Levine reached Adaline's station, she listened attentively as Adaline explained her project and pointed to the posterboard. But as she looked over the data, a frown creased her forehead.

"Adaline, this is very interesting," Mrs. Levine said, her voice kind but probing. "But some of these results seem unusual. Are you sure you followed the experiment correctly? And where are your plants?"

Adaline's heart raced, and her palms grew sweaty. She could feel the eyes of her classmates on her. She considered lying again, but the guilt was too much to bear. With her cheeks burning with shame, she finally spoke.

"No, Mrs. Levine. I—I faked the results. My experiment didn't work, and I didn't want to fail, so I made up the data."

A hush fell over the room as everyone stared at Adaline. She wanted to disappear, to melt into the floor and never have to face her peers again. But then Mrs. Levine did something unexpected. She placed a reassuring hand on Adaline's shoulder and smiled gently.

"Adaline, what you did was wrong, but it took a lot of courage to admit it in front of everyone. That's a lesson in integrity, and it's something to be proud of."

Adaline looked up, tears welling in her eyes, but Mrs. Levine's kind words gave her a sense of relief. Piper and a few other friends came up to her to offer words of comfort.

Another student, a girl named Marianne, stepped forward. "I also fudged my results a little," she confessed, her voice trembling. "It's really hard to get everything right."

Several other students nodded in agreement, sharing their own difficulties with their experiments. Mrs. Levine addressed the class with a warm smile. "Science is about exploration and learning, not just about getting the right answer. You shouldn't fake the results because it doesn't help anyone. If you're having trouble, you can always ask for help. That's what I'm here for."

Adaline felt a wave of relief wash over her. She had learned a valuable lesson, not just about science, but about honesty, integrity, and the importance of asking for help.

The classroom buzzed with anticipation as Mrs. Levine stepped up to the front of the room, holding the envelope that contained the name of the science fair winner. Adaline sat at her desk, her heart pounding in her chest.

Mrs. Levine smiled warmly at the class, her eyes scanning the eager faces before her. "I want to start by saying that each of you put in a lot of hard work, and I'm proud of all your efforts," she began. "But as you know, there can only be one winner."

Adaline swallowed hard, her gaze flickering to Andrew who sat a few rows ahead of her. She couldn't help but feel a twinge of envy, but she quickly pushed it aside. After all, she had learned the hard way that honesty was more important than winning. If she had only been honest about the results, even if they were unremarkable, perhaps she could have won.

Mrs. Levine slowly opened the envelope, the suspense in the room palpable. "And the winner of this year's science fair is Andrew Roberts, for his project on electromagnetism!"

The room erupted in applause, and, as she watched Andrew rise to accept his award, Adaline remembered the lesson she had learned. Andrew had worked hard on his project, and he deserved to be recognized for it.

As the applause died down, Mrs. Levine motioned for Andrew to say a few words. He stepped forward. "Thank you so much, Mrs. Levine. It was a tough competition, and I'm glad I could be a part of it."

Adaline made up her mind. She wasn't going to let her jealousy get the better of her. She walked over to where Andrew was packing up his project.

"Congratulations, Andrew" Adaline said, her voice steady and sincere.

Andrew looked up, a bit surprised by her approach. "Thanks, Adaline," he replied, his grin widening. But then he paused and said, "I wasn't sure I was going to make it this year. My experiment almost didn't work."

Adaline raised an eyebrow. "Really? But your project looked perfect."

Andrew shrugged, all traces of cockiness slipping away. "It wasn't at first. I had to redo the experiment a few times before it finally worked out. I was ready to give up more than once."

Adaline hesitated, then decided to take the plunge. "I've been having a lot of trouble with my experiment too. I guess that's why I did what I did."

Andrew nodded, his expression turning more thoughtful. "It happens. Science is tricky. Do you want to know why your experiment didn't work?"

Adaline blinked, taken aback by his offer. At first, her pride flared up—she wanted to refuse, to figure it out on her own. But then she remembered the lesson she had learned earlier that day. Asking for help wasn't a weakness- it was a strength.

"Yeah, I would," she said, smiling slightly. "If you have time, could you show me what I did wrong?"

Andrew's grin returned, this time without a hint of smugness. "Sure. I can come over to your house and look at the plants after school if that's okay."

Adeline nodded, feeling a sense of relief wash over her. "That would be great. Let me just ask my parents."

Later that afternoon, Andrew went to Adaline's house. They looked at her experiment still going on in the living room, and Andrew carefully examined the setup.

"Here's where you went wrong," he said after a moment. "Your light sources were too close to the plants. They need to be further away to simulate natural sunlight properly."

Adaline watched closely as Andrew adjusted the lights. She knew she wouldn't see the results right away, but she trusted him and would wait to see them later.

"That's incredible!" she exclaimed. "I didn't even think about that."

Andrew smiled, clearly pleased with her reaction. "It's all about trial and error. Sometimes it takes a few tries to get it right."

Adaline couldn't help but feel a newfound respect for Andrew. He wasn't just her rival—he was someone who understood the frustrations and joys of science as much as she did. "Thanks for helping me, Andrew. I really appreciate it."

"No problem," Andrew replied, his grin turning into a genuine smile. "We're all just trying to figure things out, right?"

As they packed up their notebooks, Adaline felt a sense of accomplishment that had nothing to do with winning. She learned that success achieved through deceit was hollow and that facing the consequences of her actions was the right thing to do. She had also made a new friend in the process.

Adaline realized something she hadn't expected: she was happy. Although she hadn't won the science fair, she had gained much more—a sense of integrity, a new friend, and a deeper understanding of what true success is. She had learned that success wasn't about beating someone else; it was about doing your best, learning from your mistakes honestly, and helping others along the way. And that, she realized with a smile, was the true victory.

> *Adaline learned that true success comes from honesty, perseverance, and helping others. When her science experiment didn't go as planned, she initially faked her results but later confessed. Because of her integrity, she gained a new friend and a deeper understanding of what it means to be truly successful. This story shows the importance of doing your best and learning from mistakes.*

Heritage and Heart

Kai Liu Zhang sat at her desk, absentmindedly curling her shoulder-length black hair around her finger. Her black eyes were focused on her best friend, Mei, who sat beside her, doodling in her notebook. The classroom buzzed with excitement as their teacher, Ms. Perez, introduced their next project.

"Class, we have two exciting activities coming up," Ms. Perez announced. "First is an ancestry project in which you'll research your family background, and second is a school-wide food drive to help local families in need."

Kai's heart sank a little. While she loved the idea of the food drive, the ancestry assignment made her feel anxious. At 11 years old, she felt disconnected from her Chinese heritage and was unsure where to start. Mei, sensing her friend's unease, nudged her gently.

"Kai, this could be fun! We can learn a lot about our families," Mei said with encouragement.

Kai managed a small smile. "Maybe, but I don't know much about my family's background. I'm feeling a bit nervous about it."

As the bell rang, signaling the end of the day, Ms. Perez called Kai over. "Kai, I know this project might seem challenging, but I believe you'll find it rewarding. Your family has a rich history worth exploring."

Kai nodded, appreciating her teacher's confidence. "Thank you, Ms. Perez. I'll do my best."

Walking home with Mei, Kai voiced her concerns. "Mei, how do you feel about the ancestry project?"

Mei grinned. "I'm excited! My grandparents love telling stories about their past. We can work on our assignments together. It'll be fun!"

Kai felt a bit more hopeful. "Thanks, Mei. Maybe I can ask my parents and grandparents for help too."

Kai's mind raced. The ancestry project seemed daunting enough, and now there was a food drive too. But maybe, she thought, they didn't have to be separate endeavors.

Kai sat in her room doing her homework when she got home from school. Sighing heavily, she looked at her dog, a miniature pinscher named Boots, who was resting on her bed, and asked, "Will you do my assignment for me?" Boots looked up at her, wagged his tail, then gave a "Ra-ruff!" as his answer. Kai giggled. "I'm hoping that's a *yes*." Worry formed in her stomach the more she thought about the assignment. How would she figure out a solution for both tasks when she had no clue what to do for either? Kai felt overwhelmed with self-doubt.

That evening, Kai decided to share her concerns with her family at the dinner table. Her parents, Yuyan and Jian Zhang, and her grandparents, Nai Nai and Ye Ye, were all present. Boots lay at her feet, looking up at her with curious eyes.

"Mama, Baba, I have an ancestry project to do for school, but I don't know where to start. And there's also a food drive. I'm not sure how to manage both."

Yuyan smiled gently. "We can help with your ancestry assignment, Kai. It's a wonderful opportunity to learn about our family's history."

Jian nodded. "As for the food drive, perhaps we can combine it with the other one. How about preparing traditional Chinese meals to share with the neighborhood?"

Kai's eyes lit up. "That sounds perfect! But I still need to learn more about our family's background."

Nai Nai, her grandmother, placed a hand on Kai's shoulder. "Let us tell you about our ancestors, Kai. You come from a long line of strong, resilient people. Our family history is rich with stories of courage and perseverance."

"Tell me, Nai Nai, where did our family come from?" Kai asked eagerly.

Nai Nai smiled warmly. "Our family comes from a small village in the Guangdong Province. Your great-great-grandparents were farmers, and they worked very hard to provide for the family. They grew rice and vegetables, and they also raised chickens."

Ye Ye chimed in, "Your great-grandfather moved to Hong Kong for better opportunities. He started a small business selling traditional Chinese medicines. That's where your grandfather and I lived before moving to America."

Kai scribbled down notes as they spoke, feeling a growing sense of connection to her family's history. "What about traditions? Are there any special customs or recipes passed down in our family?"

Nai Nai's eyes sparkled. "Oh, yes! We have many traditions, especially around food. During Lunar New Year, we make dumplings and sticky rice cakes. Your favorite, Kai, the red bean buns, were your great-grandmother's specialty."

Kai's eyes lit up. "I love red bean buns! Can you teach me how to make them?"

Yuyan smiled at her daughter's enthusiasm. "That's a wonderful idea, Mom. We can make some together and share them at the food drive."

Kai felt a growing sense of pride and connection to her family's past. She decided to incorporate these stories into her ancestry assignment She also thought about the food drive and how she could share her culture through traditional Chinese dishes.

The next few days were filled with bustling activity. Yuyan and Kai spent their evenings learning traditional recipes from Nai Nai. Boots watched curiously as Kai kneaded dough and mixed fillings, his tail wagging in anticipation of any scraps that might fall.

"Boots, no eating the dough!" Kai laughed, gently nudging her dog away from the counter. "Ra-ruff!" He then trotted around the kitchen, sniffing at the delicious aromas.

Yuyan guided Kai through each step, explaining the significance of the ingredients and the history behind the dishes. "These red bean buns symbolize prosperity and good fortune. Sharing them with others is a way to spread joy and blessings."

Kai nodded thoughtfully. "I want to share our traditions with everyone at the food drive. Maybe it will bring them some happiness too."

As they cooked, Kai also worked on her ancestry project. She created a family tree, complete with photos and stories shared by her grandparents. She felt a growing sense of pride and belonging with each new discovery.

The day of the food drive arrived, and Kai felt excited *and* nervous. The school gymnasium hummed with activity as students, parents, and teachers set up tables and organized donations. Kai and her mom carefully arranged their table with traditional Chinese dishes: red bean buns, dumplings, and sticky rice cakes. A sign read, "A Taste of Chinese Heritage."

Kai spotted her friend, Emma, across the room and waved. She'd always loved Emma's blond ringlets. Emma came over, her bright blue eyes widening at the sight of the food. "Wow, Kai! This looks amazing! Did you make all of this?"

Kai beamed with pride. "Yes, with help from my mom and grandparents. These are traditional Chinese dishes. Do you want to try some?" It shocked her that Emma was taking such an interest. Some of her other friends came over and tried the food too, and Kai felt incredible pride as she explained their origins.

Emma eagerly picked up a red bean bun and took a bite. "This is delicious! I had no idea your family had such cool traditions."

Kai felt a warm glow of pride. "Thanks, Emma. I'm learning a lot about my family's history, and it feels really good to share it with others."

As the food drive continued, more people stopped by Kai's table, curious about the dishes and their stories. She watched as people approached, curious about the unfamiliar foods. "Hello," Kai greeted them warmly. "Would you like to try some dumplings, red bean buns, and sticky rice cakes? These are traditional Chinese dishes, and my family and I made them together." Kai shared her family's history and traditions with everyone who asked, feeling more connected to her family's past with each conversation.

One woman smiled and took a dumpling. "These look wonderful. Thank you for sharing your culture with us."

Kai beamed. "You're welcome! I'm also working on an ancestry project for school, and I learned so much about my family's history. It's important to me to share that with others."

As the day passed, more people visited Kai's table, eager to try the food and learn about her heritage. Kai felt a deep sense of fulfillment. She was helping her neighborhood and sharing a part of herself.

It was time to present her ancestry project to the class the following week. Kai stood before the room, her family tree and photos displayed behind her.

"Hello, everyone. My name is Kai Liu Zhang, and I learned about my family's history and traditions for my ancestry assignment. My family comes from Guangdong Province in China, and we've kept many of our traditions alive through food. I also helped with the school food drive by sharing some traditional Chinese dishes, like red bean buns, dumplings, and sticky rice cakes. It was a way for us to give back and share our heritage with others. I've learned that discovering your roots gives you a sense of pride, and giving back to the community is a meaningful way to share your culture."

She glanced at her notes, feeling a surge of confidence. "This project taught me a lot about my heritage and made me feel closer to my family. When we share where we come from, we enrich our lives and the lives of those around us."

The class applauded, and Kai felt a deep sense of accomplishment. Ms. Perez smiled and said "Well done, Kai. Your project is an excellent example of how personal history and community service can go together."

After school, Kai walked home, feeling a new sense of connection to her heritage. She realized that celebrating her roots and helping others were powerful ways to enrich her life and the lives of those around her.

That evening, Kai and her family gathered for dinner. The table was filled with the delicious dishes they had made together. Boots sat at Kai's feet, hoping for a bite of his favorite red bean bun. "Everybody cheered after my presentation today," Kai said happily.

Nai Nai and Ye Ye approached, wrapping Kai in a warm embrace. "You did a wonderful job, Kai," Nai Nai said. "Your ancestors would be proud."

Kai smiled, feeling a warm sense of belonging. "Thank you, Nai Nai. I couldn't have done it without all of you. Thank you for helping me discover our history. I've learned that knowing where you come from and helping others are both important. It's like sharing a piece of ourselves with the world."

Yuyan nodded in agreement. "And it's a lesson that will stay with you forever, Kai."

Kai nodded, understanding the lesson deeply.

As they enjoyed their meal, Kai looked around at her family, feeling grateful for the journey they had taken together. She had discovered her heritage and found a way to give back, realizing that both were essential to her identity.

As the weeks passed, Kai volunteered at local events, sharing her family's traditions and stories. She also began to teach her classmates about Chinese culture and help them appreciate the beauty and richness of her heritage.

One day, while walking Boots in the park, Kai noticed a group of children playing together. She approached them with a smile.

"Hi, I'm Kai. Would you like to learn how to make paper lanterns? It's a tradition in my family."

The children eagerly agreed. She reached in her backpack and pulled out the supplies they needed. Soon, they were all sitting together, creating colorful lanterns and listening to Kai's stories about the Lantern Festival.

Right before the sun set, the lanterns almost looked liked they were glowing from the yellow light of the sky. Kai watched the children laugh and play and felt a deep sense of fulfillment. She had discovered her roots and found a way to share them with others, enriching her own life and the lives of those around her.

Kai knew that celebrating her heritage and helping her neighborhood were intertwined. By embracing both, she had found a way to honor her ancestors and make a positive impact on the world.

Looking down at Boots, who wagged his tail happily, Kai whispered, "We did it, Boots. We found a way to give back. And this is just the beginning."

With a heart full of pride and a spirit ready to serve, Kai Liu Zhang walked forward, ready to continue her journey of discovery and community service.

Kai learned that embracing her heritage and helping her community are powerful ways to enrich her life and the lives of those around her. By combining her ancestry assignment with the school food drive, she discovered the importance of sharing her culture and giving back. This experience taught her that celebrating her heritage and serving others go hand in hand.

Stand Tall

Fiona Callahan stood at the corner of West 87th Street and Columbus Avenue, gripping her schoolbooks tightly to her chest. Her vibrant, curly red hair danced in the morning breeze, framing her freckled face. She was tall with green eyes. Fiona's heart raced as she looked down the street toward Riverside Elementary, the school she had attended since moving to Manhattan in September. It was now February, and her 10th birthday had come and gone, yet every day felt like a new battle.

"Ready, Fiona?" her best friend Heidi asked, adjusting her oversized glasses. Heidi was extremely short for her age; her glasses covered half her face.

"Aye, ready as I'll ever be," Fiona replied, her thick Irish accent evident. She tried to muster up a brave smile for her two best friends, but anxiety had clawed its way into her.

Sarah, who had thick brown hair down to her waist and was a bit overweight, gave Fiona a reassuring nod. "We'll stick together, right? Like always." Her voice trembled as if she didn't believe her own words.

"Aye, we will," Fiona affirmed, glancing at Heidi and Sarah.

As they walked through the school gates, Fiona could see Kyle, Derek, and Jack already waiting by the playground, smirking. Kyle, the ringleader, was tall and habitually flicked his hair back whenever he was about to say something mean.

"Look who it is," Kyle sneered as they approached. "The freckle-faced leprechaun and her sidekicks."

Fiona stepped forward, standing as tall as her 10-year-old frame allowed, and shakily said "Why are ye bothering us?" Her voice was quiet and she looked at the ground as she spoke.

Jack laughed, turning toward Fiona. "Maybe when you learn to speak like the rest of us, ye, we'll stop bothering you" Sometimes, Fiona felt like her thick Irish accent was a curse.

"Maybe we just don't like the way you look," Derek chimed in.

Heidi started to walk away and Kyle grabbed her glasses from her face, placed them on the ground, and kicked them with his foot. "Good luck finding those, four eyes."

Heidi shook her head and squinted. She looked like she was going to cry but held it in.

Fiona's stomach twisted but she said nothing.

"Give us your lunches NOW," said Derek. The girls looked at each other and then pulled out their sandwiches, handing them over. The boys snickered and walked away.

The next day, Fiona, Heidi, and Sarah met in the classroom to practice chess before class and started to strategize.

"We need to be smart about this," Fiona said, her green eyes shining with determination. "Let's pack foods they won't like. My mom can make a liver sandwich for me."

Heidi wrinkled her nose. "Gross, but a good idea. My mom can pack some weird-smelling cheese."

Sarah grinned. "And I'll bring some pickled herring. After that, they won't touch our lunches."

The classroom door banged open, and Kyle, Derek, and Jack walked in. Their eyes immediately locked onto the girls. Fiona felt a familiar knot of anxiety twist in her stomach. All she wanted to do was cry.

"Well, well, if it isn't Freckles, Shorty, and Fatso," Kyle sneered, leading the pack toward them.

Fiona stood up but was too scared to say anything. Her heart pounded.

"Whatcha gonna do?" Jack taunted, knocking the chess pieces off Fiona's desk. "Gonna cry to your mammy?"

Fiona clenched her fists, resisting the urge to fight them physically. Derek grabbed Sarah's lunch from her desk and tossing it to Kyle. "We like your lunches. Yum yum!"

Sarah's face fell, but she stayed silent, her eyes pleading with Fiona. Fiona knew she had to be the one to say something, anything.

"I'm telling Principal Farragher," Fiona whispered unconvincingly.

"Tell him all you want," Kyle laughed. "He won't do anything."

The bell rang, and their teacher entered the room. The boys slunk back to their seats, snickering. Fiona sat down, her heart heavy. She had hoped that at some point the bullies would simply go away, but it seemed like nothing would change.

The next day at lunch, Fiona, Heidi, and Sarah were hoping to eat peacefully. Peace was rare these days.

"Heidi, how are yer glasses holdin' up?" Fiona asked, noticing the crack in one of the lenses getting bigger.

Heidi's hand flew up to adjust them. "My parents are getting tired of replacing them."

"Maybe we should actually talk to Principal Farragher," Sarah suggested, picking at her food. "He's the only one who may understand."

Fiona nodded. "Aye, we should do that sometime."

They fell quiet, eating their lunches.

"Hey, freaks," Kyle's voice cut through the silence.

"Why are you here?" Fiona said quietly, her voice a scared whisper.

"Because it's fun," Derek said, snatching Sarah's sandwich and taking a big bite. "Ew, what is this? It tastes awful."

Fiona's eyes twinkled with a hint of triumph. "My mom packed us food ye don't like. Guess ye'll have to find someone else to steal from."

Kyle's face twisted in annoyance. "We'll see about that."

The next day, the boys didn't steal any lunches, but they found other ways to make the girls' lives miserable. During recess, Derek tripped Heidi, completely breaking her glasses. Sarah started crying as and Fiona held back tears.

"Enough!" Principal Farragher's voice boomed from behind them. He had seen the whole thing. "Kyle, Derek, Jack- my office, now!"

As the boys sulked off, Principal Farragher turned to the girls. "Are you three alright?"

Heidi nodded, though tears streamed down her face. "My glasses..."

"We'll get them fixed," Mr. Farragher assured her. "But we need to talk. Come to my office after lunch."

Later, the girls sat in Mr. Farragher's office, the atmosphere tense but hopeful.

"Girls, I know it's tough, but you have to come to me when these events occur. How long has this been going on?"

The girls took some time to explain all the bullying from the three boys and how long it had gone on.

"I'm sorry this has been happening," Mr. Farragher said, his tone gentle. "I had a firm chat with those boys, and I have suspended them for three days. I will also talk to their parents. If this happens again, please come to me."

"We should have come to ye sooner," Fiona said quietly. "They keep bothering us. I want to punch them every time."

"They're nonstop," Sarah said softly. "What if it *never* stops?"

"It will," Principal Farragher said. "Keep seeking help from me and other teachers, and we will keep punishing them. Meanwhile, when they're back from suspension, if they bother you again you just need to use your words calmly with them, tell them to stop, and, if you can, walk away. It's not worth fighting them- two wrongs don't make a right. Then come to me and let me know."

Fiona nodded, absorbing his words. "What if they corner us again?"

"Standing up to bullies isn't always easy or immediate," he began. "Report every incident to me, another teacher or a parent. We're here to help you. Always stick together and try not to have lunch alone."

"Thanks, Principal Farragher," Heidi said, her voice wavering but grateful.

"One more thing," Principal Farragher added. "Change your routines. Eat lunch in different places and take different routes to class. Don't let them figure out your patterns."

The next few weeks were challenging, but Fiona, Heidi, and Sarah followed Mr. Farragher's advice. They varied their routines and stayed together.

One afternoon, as the girls were heading home, the bullies cornered them. Jack sneered at Fiona. "Nice hair, Carrot Top. And those freckles—did someone splatter paint on you?"

Fiona was ready for this moment. She stood tall and said "Leave us alone, Jack. Your words can't hurt us."

Kyle tried to trip Heidi. "Oops. Too short to see where you're going, Heidi?"

Heidi burst into tears, and Sarah tried to shield her. "Stop it! Why are you so mean?"

"Because it's fun," Derek said with a smirk.

Fiona's fists clenched, but she remembered Mr. Farragher's advice that two wrongs don't make a right. "We're not going to fight you. We just want to be left alone."

"Yeah, right," Jack scoffed. "Like we'll listen to you."

The girls walked away. They felt defeated but refused to give up.

The next day, they talked to Principal Farragher again.

"They won't stop," Fiona explained, her voice filled with frustration.

Principal Farragher frowned. "I'm sorry to hear that. I will do what I can on my end. We'll get this resolved together. I will get them suspended again."

Although the boys were suspended for another 3 days, once they returned, they were back to their old habits, cornering the girls once more as they headed to the library. This time, Fiona stood in front of her friends, her eyes blazing with determination.

"Give it a rest, Kyle," she said, her voice steady. "We're not afraid of ye anymore."

Kyle sneered but hesitated. Fiona's calm confidence seemed to unnerve him. Derek and Jack exchanged uncertain glances.

"You think you're so tough," Kyle muttered, but his words had less conviction.

"We are tough," Fiona replied. "We're not going to let ye get to us anymore."

"You think you can hide from us?" Kyle sneered. "Think again."

"We're not hidin'," Fiona said, her voice steady. "We're standin' up for ourselves."

Jack lunged forward, but Fiona stood her ground. "Stop," she said firmly. "We're not afraid of ye."

The boys hesitated, taken aback by her confidence. Derek scoffed. "Whatever. You're all freaks anyway."

Fiona felt a surge of anger but remembered Principal Farragher's words. "We're not freaks. We're friends. And we're not gonna let ye bully us anymore."

Kyle glared at them, but his eyes flickered with uncertainty. "Come on, guys," he muttered. Let's go."

The boys glared at them but eventually walked away, muttering under their breaths. As the boys left, Fiona let out a breath she hadn't realized she was holding. Heidi and Sarah hugged her tightly.

"You were amazing, Fiona," Heidi said, her voice full of admiration.

"We did it together," Fiona replied, smiling at her friends. "And we'll keep doin' it until they leave us alone."

"Do you think it's over?" Sarah asked, her voice hopeful.

Fiona shrugged. "Maybe not, but we'll keep standing up to them. Together."

Days turned into weeks, and the boys' bullying began to wane. The boys still made the occasional snide comments, but the intensity had lessened. The boys laughed when the girls walked by, but didn't come near them anymore. Fiona, Heidi, and Sarah grew more confident, their bond stronger than ever.

One sunny afternoon, as the girls sat peacefully by the playground, Fiona looked at her friends with a smile. "We did it, didn't we?"

Heidi adjusted her new glasses and nodded. "Yeah, but they still make fun of us," she reminded them.

Sarah grinned. "True, but they're leaving us alone. Besides, we're sticking together, so we'll just keep fighting them if they try again. Eventually, they'll get bored."

Fiona's heart swelled with pride. She had learned an important lesson: Standing up for yourself was crucial, even if it didn't bring immediate results. Plus, talking to a trusted adult had helped. Persistence, support, and courage made all the difference.

As they walked home that day, Fiona felt a sense of peace. Manhattan had become a little brighter and a little safer, all because three friends refused to back down, plus asked for help.

"Ready for a game of chess later?" Fiona asked, her eyes sparkling.

Heidi and Sarah laughed. "You bet!"

Fiona knew she had the strength and the friends to face whatever came next. Together, they could handle anything.

Fiona learned that standing up to bullies takes persistence, courage, and the support of true friends and trusted adults. Even when it seemed like nothing would change, Fiona and her friends stuck together, refused to back down, and found strength in their unity. Fiona discovered that facing challenges with determination and the right people by your side can make all the difference.

Facing the Fear

Leisel Zimmerman felt like her world was crashing down around her. At 12 years old, she had always been the quiet, sweet girl who preferred to stay in the background rather than draw attention to herself. She spent most of her days reading books about faraway lands and magical creatures, where the characters never had to deal with the awkwardness of growing up. But lately, her own body seemed determined to make her the center of attention, whether she wanted it to or not. She was short with blond ringlets and hazel eyes and was self-conscious of the fact that she wasn't as thin as all her friends.

Leisel stood in front of her bedroom mirror, frowning at her reflection. Her once-flat chest had started to fill out, and her mother had recently taken her shopping for bras—an experience Leisel would rather forget. The sensation of wearing a bra felt strange, and she couldn't shake the feeling that everyone at school would notice. Worse still, her hips had begun to widen, and the curves that her mother called "beautiful" only made Leisel want to hide. Liesel's mother told her that her beautiful curvy body was because of her German heritage, along with her blue eyes and dirty blond hair.

As Liesel dressed for gym class that day, she pulled on her gym clothes with a heavy heart. What used to be her favorite part of the school day had become a daily source of anxiety. The thought of running around in front of her classmates, her body jiggling in ways it never had before, was mortifying. She tried her best to stay out of sight, often pretending to tie her shoelaces just as the teacher called for volunteers to demonstrate exercises.

Today, however, Liesel's worst fears came true. She started her period right before gym class. It was the third month ever of Liesel getting her period, and her mother had already shown her how to attach a pad to her underwear. But during gym glass, the pad always seemed to move around. Liesel was so worried that the pad would accidentally fall out of her shorts, which caused her a ton of anxiety.

During class, the teacher had the class run laps around the track. Leisel kept her pace slow, hoping to blend in with the others. But then, as she rounded the corner on her third lap, she felt something shift. A cold dread settled in her stomach. Her pad had slipped. She could feel it moving, no longer in the place it was supposed to be, and she panicked.

Leisel tried to adjust it a few times as she slowed to a walk, but it was too late. A few girls nearby had noticed her odd behavior and started whispering to each other. Leisel's face burned with embarrassment. She could hear their giggles, and it felt like the sound was echoing off the walls, amplifying her shame. She wanted to disappear.

"Hey, Leisel, you okay?" one of the girls, Madison, called out with a smirk. She was standing with the popular girls; the others were Kelly, Nancy, and Andrea.

"What's the matter? You got ants in your pants?" Andrea yelled out.

"More like her big boobs hit her in the eye," Nancy called out, which brought on a fit of laughter from the four girls.

Leisel didn't answer. She kept her head down, praying for the class to end. Her heart pounded in her chest, and her eyes welled with tears. All she could think about was getting out of there. She had never felt so humiliated in her life.

When the teacher finally blew the whistle, signaling the end of class, Leisel bolted to the locker room. She could still hear the whispers and snickers behind her, each one like a dagger to her already fragile self-esteem. She quickly changed out of her gym clothes and stuffed her pad deep into the trash can, hoping no one would notice. She then put a new one on and made sure it was secure.

Leisel spent the rest of the day in a daze. She couldn't focus on her schoolwork, and the idea of facing her classmates again the next day made her stomach churn. By the time she got home, she had made up her mind: she was never going back to gym class. She would fake an illness or maybe even skip school entirely—anything to avoid the humiliation she had endured.

That evening, Leisel sat at the dinner table, pushing her food around her plate. Her mother, Annika, noticed her daughter's uncharacteristic silence.

"Leisel, sweetie, are you feeling okay?" her mother asked gently.

Leisel looked up, her eyes full of unshed tears. She had always been close to her mother, confiding in her about everything from her favorite books to her fears about growing up. But this was different. This was something she wasn't sure she could talk about, but she felt so alone and needed to talk to someone.

"Mom," Leisel began, her voice trembling, "something really embarrassing happened today at school."

Annika reached across the table and took Leisel's hand in hers. "Oh, honey, I'm sorry. Do you want to talk about it?"

Leisel hesitated, but the warmth in her mother's eyes gave her the courage she needed. She recounted the events of gym class, her voice barely above a whisper, and when she finished, she felt the tears spill over and run down her cheeks.

"I just don't want to go back to school, Mom," Leisel confessed, wiping her eyes. "Everyone was laughing at me. I don't know how I can face them again."

Annika's heart ached for her daughter. She had gone through her own awkward stages growing up and knew how painful it could be. She pulled Leisel into a comforting embrace.

"Leisel, I know it feels like the end of the world right now, but I promise you, it's not," Annika said softly. "These things happen to everyone, especially when you're going through changes like you are."

Leisel looked up at her mother, her eyes searching for reassurance. "Did—did anything like this ever happen to you?"

Annika smiled, a nostalgic look crossing her face. "Oh, absolutely. I remember one time in middle school, I had just gotten my period, and I was so nervous about it. I thought I had everything under control, but during math class, I realized I had leaked through my white pants. I was mortified, Leisel. I thought I would die of embarrassment."

Leisel's eyes widened. "What did you do?"

"Well," Annika continued, "I wrapped my sweater around my waist and tried to hide it the best I could. But then, a classmate noticed and pointed it out. I wanted to crawl under my desk and never come out."

Leisel's mouth dropped open. "That's awful, Mom! What happened after that?"

"I ran to the bathroom and cried," Annika admitted. "But when I got home, I talked to my mom about it, and she told me something that really helped. She said that growing up can be messy and awkward, and everyone goes through embarrassing moments like that. It doesn't define you. What defines you is how you handle it afterward."

Leisel listened intently, absorbing every word. "So, what should I do, Mom?"

Annika took a deep breath and chose her words carefully. "First of all, I think you need to give yourself some grace- periods are healthy, normal, and natural. What happened today was unfortunate, but it doesn't mean everyone will remember it forever. Kids can be mean sometimes, but most of the time, they're just trying to deal with their own insecurities. Tomorrow, if you act like it's no big deal, chances are they'll forget about it soon enough."

Leisel nodded slowly, still unsure but willing to trust her mother. "But what about gym class? I don't know if I can go back."

"I understand that, sweetheart," Annika said, stroking Leisel's hair. "But you shouldn't let one bad experience keep you from doing the things you enjoy. Here's what we can do. I'll show you some ways to make sure your pad stays in place during gym class. We can even try using different kinds of products and different pad sizes until you find what works best for you."

Leisel bit her lip. "Do you really think that'll help?"

"I do," Annika said confidently. "And if you ever feel unsure, you can always come to me. We'll figure it out together. You're not alone in this, Leisel."

The warmth and love in her mother's voice made Leisel feel a little better. She knew her mom was right— running away from her problems wasn't the answer. Maybe, just maybe, she could face her fears and get through this.

The next morning Leisel woke up and her stomach immediately twisted with anxiety. She had spent the evening talking with her mother, learned how to use a tampon, trying out different size pads, and practicing how to discreetly adjust her pad if needed. Her mom even shared a few more stories from her own teenage years, which made Leisel feel a little less alone in her struggles.

As Leisel walked into the school building, she felt a flutter of nerves in her stomach. But she reminded herself of her mother's words: Everyone goes through embarrassing moments. It doesn't define you.

When it was time for gym class, Leisel took a deep breath and joined her classmates. She noticed Madison and the other girls from the previous day whispering to each other again, and for a moment, her confidence wavered. But then she squared her shoulders, deciding she wouldn't let them get to her.

As they started their warm-up exercises, Leisel kept an eye on herself, making sure everything was in place. She followed the tips her mother had given her, and, to her relief, everything seemed fine. The whispers continued, but Leisel ignored them and focused on her own movements.

When they began to run laps, Leisel felt a twinge of fear. What if it happened again? But she pushed the thought aside and kept going. With each step, her confidence grew. She could do this. She was prepared.

After gym class ended, Leisel went to the locker room with a sense of relief. She had made it through without any disasters. As she changed back into her regular clothes, she overheard Madison talking to another girl.

"Did you see Leisel today? She seemed totally fine," Madison said, almost sounding disappointed.

"Yeah, I thought she'd freak out again, but she didn't," the other girl replied.

Leisel smiled to herself. They had expected her to crumble, but she hadn't. She had faced her fears and come out stronger on the other side. Maybe gym class wasn't so scary after all.

When Leisel got home that afternoon, her mother waited for her in the kitchen. "How was your day, sweetie?" Annika asked, handing Leisel a glass of lemonade.

Leisel grinned. "It was great! I did everything you said, and the other girls were still talking about me behind my back, but I didn't let that bother me, and then they stopped. Mom, they stopped!"

"That's terrific, Leisel," Annika exclaimed. "Seeking advice and support from trusted adults, such as me," her mother smiled and winked, "can really help you find solutions and support through tough times. I'm so proud of you honey."

As her mother hugged her, Leisel thought about how she had dealt with the situation and felt confident that she could handle almost anything as long as she faced her fears and kept trying. Leisel also realized how relieved she was that she'd opened up to her mom, who really helped her. She couldn't stop grinning for the rest of the night.

Leisel learned that growing up comes with challenges and awkward moments, but facing them with courage and support makes all the difference. By listening to her mother's advice and staying strong, she discovered that she could handle anything, even the toughest situations. For any girl reading, remember: You're stronger than you think, and seeking help when needed is a sign of true strength.

The Power of Pause

Sidney Rosewell stared at her meticulously organized calendar with a frown. Every square inch of it was filled with activities, clubs, practices, and study sessions. There was no time for anything unplanned. Her marks at school were in the high 90s, and she was determined to become a brain surgeon someday. But lately, something felt off. Sidney wasn't sure what the issue was, but a sense of unease had settled in her chest.

At lunchtime, Sidney went into the bathroom and studied her reflection in the mirror, trying to find out what was wrong with her. Tired light green eyes stared back at her. She looked at her long, straight blond hair and wondered if she should get her hair cut really short. It would take less time to maintain if it were above her ears and free her up to do more things. She smiled and returned to join her best friend Robin Hart in line at the school cafeteria.

Robin sat across from her several minutes later, munching on a sandwich. "You look stressed, Sidney," Robin observed, her eyes full of concern.

"I'm fine," Sidney replied, her voice tight. "I just have so much to do. Science club, math club, chess club, Girl Scouts... not to mention baseball and lifeguard practice. And I have to keep up with my reading too."

Robin raised an eyebrow. "You're always busy. Do you ever just, you know, take a break?"

Sidney sighed, rubbing her temples. "There's no time for breaks, Robin. If I take a break, I'll fall behind. Everyone's counting on me."

Robin reached across the table and gently placed her hand over Sidney's. "Maybe you should pick your favorite activities and let the others go. It's okay to slow down, you know."

Sidney shook her head vehemently. "No, I can't do that. Everyone needs me. And besides, what if I miss something important?"

Robin sighed, knowing it was pointless to argue with Sidney when she was in this mood. "Just don't forget to take care of yourself, okay? You're not a machine."

Sidney nodded absentmindedly, her mind already drifting to her next task. But Robin's words lingered, and a small seed of doubt grew in the back of her mind.

Later that evening, Sidney was in her room, surrounded by textbooks and notes. She was in the middle of solving a complex math problem when her mother's voice called up the stairs.

"Sidney! Dinner's ready!"

Sidney frowned at the interruption. She was in the zone, and the last thing she wanted was to stop for dinner. "I'll take my plate up here!" she called back, already grabbing her pencil to continue her work.

A few moments later, her mother, Lila, appeared in the doorway with a stern expression. "No, Sidney. We're all eating together tonight."

Sidney looked up in surprise. "But Mom, I have so much to do—"

"And it can wait," Lila said firmly. "Your father and I have decided that we're starting a new tradition. We're going to have dinner together as a family once a week, and I expect you to be there."

Sidney's heart sank. This was going to mess up her entire schedule. "But Mom, I can't! I have so much on my plate already—"

Lila held up a hand to stop her. "I know you're busy, Sidney. But family is important, and you have to make time for us too. So, please, come downstairs."

Sidney reluctantly followed her mother to the dining room, where her father, Carmen, and her younger brother, Evan, were already seated. Her older sister, Carly, was putting down her phone as Sidney sat down. Sidney's face clearly showed she would rather be elsewhere.

The dinner started off quietly, with Sidney eating as fast as she could. Her mind raced with everything she still needed to do, and she barely heard the conversation around her.

"Sidney, slow down," her father said gently. "You don't need to rush."

"But I have so much to do," Sidney mumbled through a mouthful of food.

"Well, you're not leaving this table until everyone's finished eating," Carmen said with a finality that made Sidney's stomach twist.

Sidney groaned inwardly. This was going to be torture. She watched in dismay as everyone ate at a leisurely pace, seemingly oblivious to the time ticking away.

Finally, Sidney couldn't take it anymore. "Why are you all eating so slowly?" she blurted out, her frustration spilling over.

Her mom gave her a patient smile. "We're enjoying our meal, Sidney. And we'd like you to enjoy it with us."

Sidney bit back a retort and forced herself to sit quietly until everyone was finished. As soon as they were done, she bolted from the table and rushed back to her room, her heart pounding. This new dinner tradition was going to ruin everything!

The next day, Sidney vented her frustrations to Robin during their lunch break. "I can't believe my parents are making me do this! It's such a waste of time."

Robin listened patiently, nodding along. "I get it, Sidney. But maybe it's not such a bad thing. I mean, I eat with my parents every night from Sunday to Thursday. It's nice to catch up with them."

Sidney looked at Robin skeptically. "I had no idea you ate with them almost every night. You like it?"

Robin shrugged. "Yeah, it's nice. We talk about our day and stuff like that. It's a great way to stay connected."

Sidney thought about Robin's words a week later as she sat at the dinner table with her family again. She decided to give Robin's advice a try so she asked her dad about his day at work.

Her dad's eyes lit up as he started to talk about a new project he was working on. Sidney listened, genuinely interested, and found herself asking more questions. Carly chimed in with a funny story about something that happened at school, and even Evan shared a bit about his hockey practice.

To Sidney's surprise, the dinner was actually enjoyable. She found herself laughing at Carly's jokes and getting excited about her father's project. For the first time in a long time, Sidney felt a sense of connection with her family.

As the weeks passed, Sidney began to look forward to the family dinners. She learned so much about her parents and siblings- things she never would have known if she had stayed holed up in her room. She discovered that her mother had a passion for gardening and that her father was an excellent cook. It turned out that Carly was not simply obsessed with makeup and boys— she was actually funny and had a sharp wit that Sidney hadn't noticed before. Even Evan surprised her with his sports knowledge and dedication to his hockey team.

Slowly, Sidney began to reevaluate her priorities. She realized that while she loved all of her activities, she didn't need to do them all. She dropped a few that she didn't enjoy as much and found that she had more time to spend with her family.

She started going on nature walks with Carly, who turned out to be a great hiking companion. They would talk about everything and nothing, and Sidney found herself opening up in ways she never had before. She also started tossing a baseball around with Evan in the backyard, which became a fun way to unwind after a long day.

Sidney even took an interest in her father's work and her mother's gardening. She helped cook with her father and found that cooking was quite relaxing,. When she gardened with her mother, she found that gardening was a peaceful escape from the chaos of her busy life.

One evening, as they all sat down for dinner, Sidney looked around the table at her family and felt content. She realized how much she had come to value these moments with them.

"I'm grateful for these dinners," Sidney said suddenly, surprising herself and everyone else.

Her dad smiled at her, pride in his eyes. "We're grateful to have you here with us, Sidney."

Her mom reached across the table and squeezed Sidney's hand. "It means a lot to us that you've been making time for our family."

Sidney nodded, a lump forming in her throat. She hadn't realized how much she had missed out on by always being so focused on her activities. Now, she couldn't imagine life without these dinners.

Months passed, and Sidney continued to make time for her family. She excelled in school and still aimed to become a brain surgeon one day, but she was no longer driven solely by the need to achieve. She had learned to appreciate the simple, everyday moments that brought her closer to the people she loved.

One evening, after dinner, Sidney sat out on the porch with her father and watched the sunset.

"You've grown up a lot, Sidney," Carmen said. "I'm really proud of you."

Sidney smiled up at him. "Thanks, Dad. I've learned a lot this year."

He put his arm around her shoulders, and they sat in comfortable silence, watching as the sky turned shades of pink and orange.

Sidney had always been smart and driven. But now she understood that true wisdom wasn't just about knowing things—it was about understanding the value of family, the importance of gratitude, and the beauty of the world around her.

As she looked out at the horizon, Sidney felt a deep sense of peace. She still had big dreams and wanted to achieve great things, but now she knew that the journey was just as important as the destination. She was grateful to have her family by her side every step of the way.

Sidney's story teaches us that, while pursuing dreams and keeping up with your work is important, it's equally crucial to make time for family and self-care. By slowing down and connecting with her loved ones, Sidney discovered that balance brings true fulfillment. Prioritizing relationships and appreciating simple moments can enrich your life and make the journey toward your goals even more meaningful.

Changing Her Tune

Polly McFadden was not one to blend in, even if she tried. With her bright, thick red hair that practically glowed in the sunlight, green eyes that sparkled with curiosity, and a face full of freckles, she was a sight to behold. Standing tall for her age, she was also lanky and had the kind of uncoordinated movements that made her seem perpetually on the brink of a tumble. Burlington, Vermont, was a far cry from the small Scottish village she had called home just a few months before, and now, at 12 years old, Polly was trying to fit into the complex world of middle school in a brand-new city.

"Ye'll do just fine," her mother had reassured her that morning as Polly stood nervously by the front door, her backpack hanging loosely over one shoulder. "Jest be yerself, lass."

But being herself wasn't as simple as it sounded, especially when "being herself" meant tripping over her own feet in front of her classmates or accidentally spilling her lunch tray in the cafeteria. Polly had learned quickly that middle school wasn't a place where clumsiness was easily forgiven. So she kept to herself, hoping to go unnoticed.

That was until she met Tamara.

Tamara was a whirlwind of energy and confidence, the kind of girl who could light up a room just by walking into it. She had short, curly hair, dark brown skin, and an infectious smile that seemed to melt away any of Polly's shyness.

"Hi! You're new here, right?" Tamara had asked on Polly's second day, practically bouncing over to her during recess.

Polly nodded, not trusting herself to say much.

"Cool! I'm Tamara. You should totally join some after-school activities with me. It's a great way to meet people and, you know, find your thing!"

Polly blinked at her. "M-me?"

"Yes, you! C'mon, it'll be fun. There's jazz, tap, ballet, gymnastics, clubs... You name it, we've got it! You just have to try things out and see what fits."

Polly wasn't sure anything would fit, but Tamara's enthusiasm was hard to resist. Before she knew it, Polly found herself signing up for more activities than she'd ever dreamed of.

First up was dance. Polly wasn't entirely convinced this was a good idea, given her tendency to trip over her own two feet, but she figured it was worth a shot. Maybe, just maybe, she'd find some hidden grace within herself.

The reality of jazz class hit her like a ton of bricks. Within the first 10 minutes, Polly had managed to collide with three other students, tangle herself in the ribbons of her jazz shoes, and somehow end up flat on her back, staring at the ceiling.

"Are you okay?" Macy, a girl with short blonde hair and big blue eyes, asked, offering her a hand to pull herself up up.

Polly accepted the hand, her cheeks flushing with embarrassment. "Aye, just need tae work on me landin', I suppose."

Macy laughed, and Polly found herself smiling despite her bruised ego. Maybe she wasn't cut out for jazz, but at least she had made a new friend.

Next, Polly tried tap, which was even worse. The rhythm was impossible to follow, and every time she tapped her toes, she ended up kicking the person in front of her.

"Sorry! Sorry!" Polly muttered repeatedly, her face burning even redder than usual.

Ballet was no better. Her lanky limbs refused to move in sync with the graceful girls around her, and the instructor's constant corrections only made her more self-conscious. Polly couldn't help but feel like a giraffe in a room full of swans.

Gymnastics, she quickly discovered, was a no-go as well. Polly had barely managed a forward roll when she smacked her elbow on the mat and winced in pain.

"Maybe this isn't for me," Polly said to herself as she nursed her bruised arm.

But she kept going. If there was one thing Polly was good at, it was perseverance. She joined the chess club, only to find the strategies baffling. The science club was fun, especially when it came to the experiments, but she felt out of her depth when discussions got too technical. The computer club was boring, though she did meet a boy named Greg who was kind and always treated her nicely.

One afternoon, while sitting alone at lunch, Polly saw Tamara approaching with a tray full of food and an even bigger smile.

"How's it going, Polly? Found your thing yet?"

Polly sighed. "Not yet, Tamara. It seems like I'm hopeless at everything."

Tamara shook her head vigorously. "No way! You're just exploring. You'll find something that makes you happy. I'm sure of it."

Polly wanted to believe her, but her confidence was wearing thin. That afternoon, she walked into the newspaper club, thinking it might be her last attempt before giving up entirely. The club advisor, Mrs. Peters, assigned her to the poetry column, and Polly hesitated. She had never thought of herself as a writer, let alone a poet.

"Give it a try," Mrs. Peters encouraged. "You might surprise yourself."

To Polly's shock, she did. Words flowed out of her like they'd been waiting for the right moment. She crafted a poem about a redheaded girl lost in a forest, searching for a place to belong. Mrs. Peters praised her work, and for the first time since moving to Burlington, Polly felt a glimmer of pride.

Her real moment of discovery came by accident, as so many things in Polly's life did. One day, as she was leaving school, she heard the most beautiful music floating through the hallway. The sound was warm and rich and seemed to vibrate in the air around her. Polly followed the music to the source, finding herself at the door of the music room.

Peeking inside, she saw students playing various instruments, but her eyes were drawn to one in particular—a cello. The student playing it was swaying gently with the music, and the deep, resonant notes made Polly's heart ache in the best way possible.

She stood there for several minutes, entranced, until the music stopped, and the students began to pack up.

"Hey, are you interested in joining the music club?" a voice asked from behind her. Polly jumped, turning to find a tall girl with fiery red hair much like her own. "I'm Lucy. I play the harp."

Polly nodded, her voice catching in her throat. "Aye, I think I'd like that if it's not too late."

Lucy grinned. "It's never too late! What instrument are you thinking about?"

Polly's gaze drifted back to the cello. "That one. It's... beautiful."

"Good choice!" Lucy said, her eyes lighting up. "Why don't you talk to Mr. Ellis, the music teacher? I'm sure he'd love to have you in the club."

That night, Polly could barely contain her excitement. As soon as she got home, she rushed into the kitchen where her mother was preparing dinner.

"Mum, can I join the music club? I want to learn the cello!"

Her mother paused, setting down the knife she was using to chop vegetables. "The cello? That's a lovely instrument, Polly. Aye, and it reminds me of yer grandpa. Did ye know he used to play in an orchestra?" Her mother smiled warmly, a hint of sadness in her eyes. "Aye, he did. He'd be so proud tae see ye followin' in his footsteps."

Polly's heart swelled. "So can I join?"

"Of course ye can, lass. Ye'll need tae practice a lot, though."

"That's fine! I'll practice every day!"

Polly's little brother Finn snorted from the living room. "Good luck with that, Polly. Ye're clumsy enough as it is. Ye'll probably end up breakin' it!"

Polly stuck her tongue out at him but ignored his teasing, too excited to let it bother her. After dinner, her mother sat down with her, and they talked about her new musical venture. Polly felt a connection to her grandfather she hadn't felt since he passed away two years earlier.

The next day, Polly approached Mr. Ellis after school. He was a kind, middle-aged man with graying hair and glasses that constantly slipped down his nose.

"I'd like tae join the music club and learn the cello," Polly said, trying to keep her nerves in check.

Mr. Ellis smiled. "We'd be happy to have you, Polly. The cello is a wonderful instrument. Do you have one, or will you need to borrow one from the school?"

Polly hesitated. "I dinnae have one yet."

"No problem. We have a spare. Let's get you started."

And so, Polly began her lessons. The cello was harder to play than she had imagined, and, at first, the notes she produced were more screeches than music. But she was determined, and, with each practice session, she improved a little more.

One afternoon, as she went to her room to practice the borrowed cello from the music room, she noticed another cello in the corner of the room with a bow on top of it and a small note from her parents:

"We found Grandpa's cello. It's yours now. Practice times are on the schedule below so ye dinnae drive us crazy. Love, Mum and Dad."

Polly's eyes filled with tears as she gently ran her fingers over the smooth wood.

Every day after school, she would hurry home, eager to practice on the old, weathered cello her parents had found at her grandmother's house—the very same one her grandfather had played.

Many months later, it was time for the concert her music club had been practicing for. Her whole family was there, including her grandmother. She could see them in the second row and waved as she went over to her cello to make sure everything was as it should be.

Half an hour later, she was playing her cello for the whole auditorium to hear. Playing the cello for an audience was an experience unlike any she had ever had. With the cello rested against her chest, its wooden body vibrating, and the bow smooth and familiar in her hand, she loved how the instrument translated her emotions into sound.

As she followed the conductor's movements, her heart pounded, not from nerves, but from the rich and full sound the cello made. As she played, the music took over, and the audience seemed to narrow to the sound of the cello as the music flowed through her, as if the cello was alive with the rich warm sound—from sorrowful, heart-wrenching melodies to joyful, exuberant bursts.

Polly realized she wasn't just playing the cello—she was part of something much larger, something magical that had the power to move hearts and stir souls. She felt like she was stirring her grandfather's soul with her music. She hadn't felt this close to him since he'd passed, and she knew he was there with her, feeling the music. She felt the connection and looked out into the crowd to see her family and all her new friends. She knew that after all her searching, she had finally found her thing! Plus, she felt comfortable with her music AND her poetry writing, so she now had multiple things!

> *Polly's story teaches us that finding where you truly belong takes time, perseverance, and an open heart. Despite initial struggles and doubts, Polly discovered her passion for the cello, love of writing, and a connection to her family. Her journey reminds us that it's okay to explore and fail before finding what that truly makes us happy and feel at home.*

Conclusion

As you close this book, take a moment to reflect on the incredible journeys you've just experienced. Each story was a reminder of the unique and powerful qualities you also possess. You've seen how girls just like you were brave in the face of fear, kind in the midst of hardship, thoughtful when making tough decisions, creative when finding solutions to their problems, and unstoppable when chasing their dreams.

Remember, the strength, courage, and wisdom you admired in these characters are qualities that you already have and can tap into. Embrace new experiences, challenge assumptions, and step boldly beyond your comfort zone.

You can accomplish great things, overcome challenges, and make a difference in the world. Never forget how special and amazing you are. The possibilities are limitless, and your heart is your greatest guide.

As you go about your days, remember that you are powerful, you are resilient, and you are enough. Let these stories be a source of light, reminding you of the incredible girl you are inside. The world is waiting for your unique spark—go out and shine!

Made in the USA
Las Vegas, NV
28 November 2024

12237470R10049